WAXWINGS

WAXWINGS

Daniel Nathan Terry

Lethe Press
Maple Shade NJ

Published by Lethe Press, 118 Heritage Ave.,
  Maple Shade NJ 08052, June 25, 2012
lethepressbooks.com   lethepress@aol.com

ISBN-13: 978-1-59021-355-1
ISBN-10: 1-59021-355-1

Cover: "Icarus 1" by Benjamin Billingsley, acrylic on canvas, 16x20, 1996
Photo: Curtis Krueger, 2012

for Ben

Acknowledgments

I would like to thank the journals in which the following poems first appeared:

"Called colored, in my youth," and "Red Horse" *Assaracus*.
"The Anhinga of Moccasin Bluff" *The Spoon River Poetry Review*.
"Scarecrow" and "The Witch's Tree" *Atlantis*.
"Lost" *Big Muddy*.
"For all of its windows" *Poet Lore*.
"Flattened Penny" and "Makeover" *New South*.
"After the Storm" *The Café Review*.
"In the Tattoo Parlor" *Weber: The Contemporary West*.

The following poems first appeared in the Seven Kitchen Press chapbook *Waxwings*:
"Wicker Man"
"Self-Portrait (Gay Son of a Preacher)"
"Since they put you out"
'He Comes to Oak Island"
"Day of the Dead, 1994"
"David, Full-Blown"
"David"
"Winter Moon"
"The Last Christmas with My Brother"
"Opening the Winter House"
"Burning the Peach"
"Waxwings"
"I Have to Have You Like She Had to Have the Rain"
"A Rumor of Fire"

I would also like to give thanks to Ron Mohring, who believed in the first incarnation of this book; to Steve Berman and Charles Jensen, who were willing to take a chance on this incarnation, to Toby Johnson for his beautiful book design; to all of those who helped shape these poems, including Lavonne Adams, Chuck Benya, Kristin Bock, Judy Bolz, Bryan Borland, Jericho Brown, Wayne Campbell, Larry Coleman, Mark Cox, David Garland, Jeff Gundy, Judy Kim, Lee Knight, Lucky, Ed Madden, Sarah Messer, Missy, Malena Mörling, Hermione, Jason Mott, Jack Myers, Ariana Nash, Trista Nicosia, Carol Peters, Kate Rusby, Ashley Shivar, Kevin Simmonds, Michael Taeckens, Andrea Terry, Christopher Phelps, Barbara Cagle-Terry, Douglass Terry, Orliss Terry, Will Tomory, Dan Vera, Michael White, Mark Wunderlich, and Winchester.

And, as always, much love and gratitude to my family.

Contents

Waxwings

I.

Scarecrow

Scarecrow crafter, burlap-tailor,
black-eye smudger, when I'm done,
crows mistake you for a man:
silent shooer, stock-still farmer,
to them alone a tartan terror.
I fisted through your flannel,
spiced your straw with artemisia,
puffed your chest with wilted-rue,
perfumed your thighs with summer sweet—
another half-attempt at love—to keep
the flies from you, who do not care
if you are flesh or straw; stand still in June,
they will devour you. If they don't and you see
the summer through, the sun, the wind, the rain
make fast work of you until your pie-pan hands
cease to flutter and the crows
begin to mutter that you can't be much.
Winter comes. Now the squash begins
to earn its name; cold snaps beans.
Like tomatoes that turn from green to glass
my red for you is missing.
How long before the snow and I
take you down?

Self-Portrait (Gay Son of a Preacher)

Old enough for evening service,
too young to stay awake, for a moment the boy
sleeps against his mother's side,

his left hand clutching the pale green hem
of her blouse. He wakes suddenly,
falling, a startling sureness

of his own destruction, his little soul
trailing his body like a failed parachute.
His father's voice opens in the waking world.

It is the voice of Jesus—deep as a baptistery.
The sermon is halfway over,
but the boy hears enough—Naaman,

once a great warrior, became a Leper,
ghost-white, his flesh a torn garment
of wounds. And he remained that way—

until he obeyed God's prophet, washed
seven times in the river Jordan and his flesh
was made clean and new as a child's.

The boy's fear slips away—he releases
his mother. He rises, joins the altar call.
His father's arms open

before him, wafer and wine in his hands,
the congregation sings "Just as I Am."
But the boy, silent, mouth open,

hears only his Savior—a voice
in his chest—saying *Come,*
and I will make you whole.

Waxwings

Waiting for the school bus at the end of the gravel drive,
eyes skyward, the boy counts thirty-seven waxwings
necklacing the telephone wire. They are too distant
to see the glistening red drops for which the birds are named,
but he knows they're there, at the tip of those folded wings
like seals on old correspondence between lovers. The cool air trills

and wheezes with strange talk. As he shifts
his backpack, one bird swoops from the wire
to the round holly pincushioned with scarlet berries
not five feet away. The boy freezes. The bird plucks one only,
then returns to the wire. Gingerly,
the berry uncrushed, the gatherer passes it to its neighbor,

who passes it in turn, and so on down the wire.
In the long minutes before the bus arrives,
the same bird gathers berries, passes them down
until each bird is satisfied. Finally, the first bird fed
feeds the provider. Sometimes the boy fantasizes
that kids in his class break into song

and dance like fools in an old musical. The camera records it
from the rafters, all of them holding hands—
Jack the football star, Shannon the beauty queen,
Ronny the bully, Todd the unattainable, the distant,
the secret, the wrong—joined together in a star of arms and legs
that kaleidoscopes in the blackness. Everyone smiles

as they mouth the words to a love song.
The bus arrives, the door sighs open,
he shoulders his books and steals one last look
at the waxwings—sated, silent. He wants to reach out,
break the red seal, open the envelopes of their wings,
read their characters on the white sky

until he understands, until they become a story
he can share.

Wicker Man

In a chair of woven willow twigs and branches of birch and ash, in the fingers of trees, interlaced and overwrought—you sit. White as a skeleton stripped from flesh, resilient and fragile as bone, the wicker back supports you better than the wingback by the hearth favored by your mother who passed away last fall, better than the La-Z-Boy your father leaves empty by choice.

Knowing you were not fully boy, you imitated girls—ignoring the obvious between your legs—selecting smooth over rough. This was before Mr. Universe told Oprah he went down on men, religiously shouting the name you would not speak, the name they spat on the playground. This was before the Salk Institute proclaimed your rapture no rarer than blue eyes, your suffering as mundane as a freckle. These absolutions came years after sermons of man and woman, lectures of sperm and egg, and casual conversations that twisted you into the delicate.

A wicker-man, now, outside. And within, the condemned—innocent and guilty, together without distinction—waiting for the torch from witch and priest alike. And it's no wonder you take punishment so willingly; if you believe the talk, you know your kind was consigned to the fire by God in the cities of the plain. And the only one who spared a thought for you was reduced to salt.

But it is late—Lot's wife and Druids in lifetimes as far away as sleep and comfort—you do not smell the ashes of friends incinerated, you do not hear the cries of those tangled in your limbs. Instead, you imagine a man from the fields, sun and pollen on his brow, exertion ripened in the hollows of his flesh, work-weary, with just the strength reserved to wrap himself around and rhythm you to sleep. You see these men in bars, place yourself in their paths, but every night they walk right through you and leave together. Later, their lips slack with lovemaking, they light each other's smokes and sit on chairs of wood.

At home, morning just hours away, you await the final conflagration in repose. The tortured canes beneath your thighs—imprinting you with pain, marking you for persecution—strangely soothing.

Called colored, in my youth,

for T.J.

they picked cucumbers in the fields around our house—
large, dark women squatted on downturned buckets
to bring the ground nearer their hands, to rest their knees.

Boys my age who should have been in school worked beside them,
paid by the bucket, shirtless and black as their mothers' brows. Afternoons,
I watched from the porch swing—the boys' slim bodies bent at the waist,

their jeans riding low on brown hips. Now and again
I was blessed with a glimpse of smooth skin that I knew
was forbidden. The Gaddys, who owned the fields,

called them *niggers*, but my mother allowed them
the use of our bathroom. The neighborhood trashed
us, said we were dirty and that they'd never touch a thing

in our house. Called us *Nigger-lovers*, said *the blackness comes off.*
Warned me not to play with the colored boys or I'd get mine.
I already knew I shouldn't want to play with those boys, shouldn't

want boys of any color the way I wanted the oldest of them—Tyrell,
fifteen, the one Miss Gaddy spat was *so black he's blue.* Tyrell
who looked like the David I conjured when my father read from the Bible.

But that near-holiness didn't stay my hardness, didn't close my mouth
as I watched him sweat and bend. I wanted to touch Tyrell, wanted
to feel the hot night I believed he carried on his back,

wanted to take him in my hand, my mouth, wanted
to find out for myself if the blackness would really come
off on my pink skin. So I did, and in some way, it did. One day

I heard screams—a copperhead, long as a broom and thick as man's
wrist found coiled beneath the umbrellas of the long cucumber vines.
Tyrell, who I believed by then I loved, rushed

to where his mother pointed while the others ran
from the field. With one iron arc of his right arm, he sliced
the snake's head off with a machete, then tossed the writhing,

bloody rope into the roadside ditch beside our house.
Days later, after I heard he'd been arrested for stealing a car,
I walked to the ditch to see my champion's kill.

Headless, it seemed alive, its body still undulating
like the sea lived inside its brown and pink skin, bucked the way I did
some nights when I came, when I woke with the dark night

dreams across my belly. A closer look exposed this false resurrection—
from the wound in its neck, I could see maggots hollowing
its body. The snake was dead, but thousands of little white lives

wouldn't let it rest.

Flattened Penny

I stand beside my sister, the parsonage lawn cool
against the arches of my feet. At seven I am half her age
and height, possess less than half her wisdom.

How far up and how far away? I ask as we stare
at a distant caravan of clouds. *So far*, she answers,
as far as France or Russia. Our neighbor push-mows his yard,

the rumble of the old engine trembles the air,
crosses the road. Oil smoke invades
me. I look down at the lawn beneath my feet,

imagine it multiplying, extending to the pavement,
sprouting like hair on walls and rooftops until it covers
the neighborhood, the town, the state, creeping its way to France

or Russia. *My teacher says Russia hates us*, my sister says
frankly, *they want to blow us all away.* She goes on
about missiles, war, communism. She mimics: *We will bury you!*

Her hand miming the pounding of a shoe. I say nothing,
look over at our neighbor's wife tearing at the ground
around their mailbox, changing the heat-worn petunias for mums.

Soon it will be fall. Finally, I mutter: *Daddy said
Jesus saved us.* My sister scruffs my hair, laughs:
That's just your soul. We all die. I keep my eyes

on the mounting pile of wilting petunias,
their pale roots desiccating in the sun. I reach
into my pocket, withdraw my lucky penny—

thumb its smoothness, remembering when we placed it
on the silver train tracks, then crouched in the runoff ditch,
the *thump-ca-chunk* of the train growing louder, the black engine

rounding the woods, the deep vibrations coursing through
our hands and knees, the gravel popping between the ties.
Then the boxcars: red, blue, faded gold, the silhouette of a monstrous

black cat. The wheels squalling past, the wind and soot
buffeting our faces. After the passing, we found the penny,
yards from where we laid it—polished bright as new copper,

thin as a holy wafer, transformed by the weight

and might of the Southern Rail, Lincoln's face erased.
I never thought to ask my sister where the train came from,
where it was going, who sent it.

Photograph, 1984

Swallow this
house—bedroom window paned
like a roadside cross
erected for a reckless boy, wreath
of camera-flare, paper flower of real grief
with too bright a center, edges finally fading
in shoebox weather.
                        You know
what happened there.
                        You know
this is more than a snap-
shot. Flat as it seems, it will swell
on your red tongue and will become
those rooms—that room with its pale boy
sinking to his knees, again, sinking
into shadowed corners.
                        Come,
fold into black origami.
                        Come, unhinge
your jaw like the copperhead you saw
becoming a blackbird in the woods—mouth-first,
then your throat, your white ribs and pink gut.
All that's left of you
                        must muscle through
the flapping wing, thin legs trembling,
one skeletal foot curling inward.
                        It's in you now—
the song, the sin, the bones, the room, him
telling you it's alright, and every man does it
when a girl leaves him empty-
handed.
        Swallow this
house, blackbird-who-became-a-snake. Swallow
this house and keep yourself
                        from remembering
how to sing.

The Anhinga of Moccasin Bluff

The slender neck of an anhinga periscopes from black water, a dark memory snaking from a darker mind, easy grace from an insatiable heart. From the canoe where we watch, the bird's body beneath the pond's skin is mythic, a thing of combinations—half-sky, half-water, oiled wings sleeked to hollow ribs in the murk, webbed feet propelling it into nurseries of brim, where it stabs and thrusts, fills its gullet, then melts into the depths.

Ten years have passed since we first paddled the narrows—rods, lures, tackle tossed into the boat, needless as the lies we might never have used. It was his doing, back in high school, his machinations—the invitation to his father's house, fishing boat capsized on sawhorses at the swamp's edge, warm beer in the mud-streaked cooler, pack of Marlboro's and a bag of weed in his pockets—everything orchestrated to coerce me into what I would have done with him anywhere. He led us downstream, past islands promising firm-footing, no more than blankets of green thrown over the water's bed, undulating with the kiss of an oar.

He brought us to the finger of rock where Lumbee boys once entered manhood with one swift dive into snake-infested blackness. In the shade of the promontory, he got high enough to dare me into nakedness, into diving, into touching him, into going down. One swift submergence in darkness to become what I already was, boat rocking beneath us. Silence and shame afterward. And in my periphery, the crooked neck of an anhinga breaking the surface, a black question in blacker shadows.

He's married now. Sons of his own fill the spaces and what once was his father's house contracts with every birth. His wife nurses the baby, watches the clock. Miles away, my suitcase waits unopened on a motel bed by the interstate that will take me north. The city. My life lived in the open. No shame even when I behave shamefully. He pops a beer, the canoe drifts toward the opposite bank. Splayed knees of cypress trees close in around us, a cordillera of wood. His voice trembles like a virgin's—*Do you remember when I dared you to dive in naked?*

I have loved more men than I choose to recall, held hands in broad daylight, nursed and buried a lover. He attends church each Sunday, takes his wife's hand as they cross the short main street that leads, eventually—no matter how often he repents—here. Now he slides his hand higher, casts his eyes down. I look out on the water. The anhinga emerges from the blackness, stands erect on a half-sunken log. Spreads its wings—a dark cloak drying in the sun, waiting for the rising heat, waiting for the updraft to give it flight.

Since they put you out

no chair receives you,
no bath invites you,
no stove pot simmers
you to supper, no mattress
gives to cradle you,
no down rises to fill
the empty spaces
your spine leaves behind
in the back-bending nightmares
you've suffered since
you got the shove. Since
you got the boot, no door
thuds protectively behind you,
no hallway echoes
without reminding you,
your feet fall too much
alone. Since they kicked you
to the curb, no memory
of mama makes you warm,
no papa's chestnut
is worth the recollection
of Sammy cracking your tooth
in the seventh grade
because you were too pretty,
too soft, too much for him—
what you did for him behind
the shed. This made the journey
from home to hell not easier,
but expected. Like a whore
you know love turns
on a dime.

II.

He comes to Oak Island

in winter's gray to elapse
the two weeks between blood drawn
and blood diagnosed.

In a shoal ahead,
a white ibis dabbles madly
in the wet sand—

its slender neck tipped
with a narrow, curved black beak
looks like a white,

skeletal arm holding
a pen of reed. He wonders
whose name it's inscribing

in the Book of the Dead.

Elegy Written in November

I. The Backward Glance
after Michael Burkard

On the way home from the store,
I thought I saw you, white bird of my childhood,
bathing in the public fountain on Market Street.

Or was it only a white paper cup floating
on the water's skin like a wish that would not drown,
even though it had been wished away?

Then this evening, again I saw your face
in the face of the tired man
buying bread and beer

at the checkout of The Village Market.
And again, just now—in the window
above the frayed, green sofa—your face

in the reflection of my face, as I searched the air,
beginning to darken, for a bird I was certain
I'd heard call out a moment before.

II. Day of the Dead, 1994

David,

before you died, our friends strung your floatation bed
with a garland of pumpkin lights in celebration of Halloween,

your favorite holiday. When Tony, our old roommate,
came to visit, you were already a skeleton—your face

a ghost's mask of morphine, your mind just earthbound enough
to pull your pale lips into a grin as you whispered: *boo*.

III. Negative

You are handsome, and still
twenty-three on the brown scroll
of negatives curled in the camera
bag's black next to *Risk*, *Monopoly*, *Life*—
board-games I will never play again,
next to worn-out dancing shoes
I would never wear now, but
refuse to throw away. So what?
I will leave you with them
on the floor of the closet.
I won't deliver you into the light
of my fortieth year. Stay where you are—
little more than a child I loved
when I was little more than a child—
almost forgotten in the closet's dark belly,
still pregnant with what is dead.

IV. Poncirus trifoliata 'Montstrosa'
Common Name: Flying Dragon

When I look at the contorted citrus tree in winter, leafless, its green limbs twisted and curled with long thorns sharp as claws, I can almost see the body of a dragon revealed in the plant's brambles. It reminds me of the ancient story about a painter so skilled, everything he created looked real enough to breathe—with one exception—the eyes of his creatures were always blank, intentionally unpainted.

The artist moved from village to village, leaving eyeless tigers and blind herons behind him on walls and vases. The Emperor, enamored with the artist's skill, demanded he paint a great dragon to curl about the walls of his palace.

The artist obliged. He created his finest work—a dragon greener than the skin of the citrus tree, each scale rendered perfectly—but with a face as eyeless as a branch. Enraged by the flaw, the Emperor demanded the eyes be painted, that his dragon be complete.

Reluctantly, the artist acquiesced. But the moment he painted the eyes, the dragon drew breath, uncoiled and flew away. And the Emperor was left with only the memory of his great dragon and its waking eyes. But even this memory would not stay. Over his long life, it faded like a procession of clouds that almost returned the faces of lost lovers, but never their eyes.

V. David, Full-blown

They say you pulled the IV from your arm, disconnected
the morphine drip, tugged your street clothes over your bones
and walked from the hospital on your own. In a daze,

you caught the downtown bus, headed home. They say
they found you curled in your bed like a child,
that they had to wake you and take you back to the hospital,

plug you in for your own safety. Out of your mind, they say.
Disoriented. As if you left the hospital for no good reason.
As if you didn't know where you were going.

VI. Heavy pumpkin

bought in October, round and bright
as the sinking sun—believe me,

                I meant to slice you

a smile so terrifying you'd make the night
moths shriek as you breathed them in

through your teeth of fire and smoke
like an idol's sacrificial throat.

                But I couldn't

bring myself to make a monster of you—
not with all the losses we'd suffered through

the fall. So I left you as you were by the garden gate
and assured myself

            I'd made a holy gesture—
not to the leering dead—but to the autumn

harvest, to the promises of rebirth and youth made
by the spring and the summer.

               Heavy pumpkin,

now it is winter and the long cold night
has picked up the knife I put down. And without

a thought, it has carved for us both—
and what's worse,
it has carved from within—a rotting mask, a death-head's
grin.

VII. David

I take it on my brow: I never loved you
while you lived. Gifts, suppers, that you brought

the quilt over my cold shoulder,
that my discomfort made you wakeful

as I slept on—these things notwithstanding—
your kisses never made me burn. I hold it in my heart:

you needed to be loved and I failed you,
that you were sick and kept it hidden,

that you chose to die as quietly as you lived,
that you reached my soul at last

through terror. I know it in the core of me:
no one deserves to be as frightened as you were

at the end, no one deserves to be afraid as I still am—
even if they are liars, cowards, slow to love, even

if to this day, they can think solely of themselves.
Right or wrong, God may brand my skin like Cain's:

I have outlived you.

VIII. The open umbrella

that threw off its owner in a fit
of envy as a crow flashed overhead,
now lingers on the curb.

Cars and trucks pass by, trailed
by the soft, beckoning hands of the wind.
Who can blame the open umbrella

for refusing a lift from these strangers—
however welcoming? But how long
is too long to wait for forgiveness

from the one who held you
in the rain? Night comes,
the umbrella's ribs blacken

beneath the starless sky. Concealed
from the moon, the umbrella's heart
beats blacker still. The open umbrella

turns into a lamp of darkness.

Winter Moon,

because you wish it
the sun sets and the wind lifts
the wings of weary birds.
You are the roost in the magnolia's
thunderhead of shadows.
You are why, half-hidden
by storm-black leaves,
the birds become silver prey
to waking owls unless they remain
more silent than stones
when they sleep. You are to blame
that strong men, tucked under
the roof of night, imagine faces
the long day helped them to forget.
And it's your fault
that they enter a sleep cluttered
with impossible,
beautiful reunions.

The Last Christmas with My Brother

Because we've no reason to doubt its existence,
we find perfection: a spruce—fragrant, wide,
ghost-green. It looms over my orange toboggan,

comes up even with my brother's eyes.
I am seven. Our dog, black and sturdy as a gun-barrel,
not yet a year old. My brother is fourteen.

I have gone with him into the woods
that stitch the snowy fields together. He pushes me back,
raises the axe and swings: the shock

of the strike echoes through the narrow woods.
Winchester barks, running the length
of the fields as if he's had a hand in the kill.

Crisp air fills the spaces the axe cleaves;
the spruce shudders into the snow. When crows
pass over, they are a ragged ellipsis

against the white day slowly disintegrating above us.
But for that moment, what will go
wrong between us, the divergent paths we will take

to find home, remains in the distance.
I reach out, catching sky in my palms
until cold invades my mittens. My brother laughs,

shouldering the axe. Grips the tree, moves on.
The dog chases field mice, oblivious,
bounding in and out of drifts ahead—

a graphite mark that keeps erasing itself.
I help my brother drag the tree; it's dying boughs
sweep our footprints clean from the snow.

The field behind us is blank as an unwritten page.

Makeover

When your sister is dying, you don't fear
death itself – although there is a moment

when you join her at the makeup counter
and imagine that death sifts from the black brush

that dusts her cheeks, then slips
easy as smoke between her parted lips –

until it coils in her breast like a decision –
and you worry: if it invaded her will it

invade me? But you don't dwell on this,
you think of time and of how long it takes

to choose a tube of lipstick, of how difficult it is
to find one pretty enough to lift her spirits.

One bright enough to draw focus from
her sallow skin and shadowed eyes.

One red enough to tear your eyes away from
the headscarf that has replaced the lovely auburn hair

you always coveted.

Opening the Winter House

The things you missed after cleaning the bedroom
for three solid hours:

on the crown of the lamp that lights the room—
a film of dust;

on the low-boy, obscured by dark grains of wood—
the black sickle of an eyelash

plucked out by nervous fingers
that forgot to make a wish;

in the blue journal—two persuasive lines
cowering in an abandoned letter;

beneath the bed-skirt—a papery egg sack that cradles
a thousand dreamless and blind soon-to-be spiders;

and on the nightstand, contained for now
in the recharging digital camera—

his smile;

and behind it—the whole of the Atlantic swells,
fostering an undertow swift enough

to sweep you out to sea.

Burning the Peach

Past the clapboard barn, the rutted road sank west into the grove of Red Haven peaches my family owned but did not care for. Snow dusted into the low beams and ahead of us a dozen fires punched holes through night's black tin. The final harvest over months before, we pulled into a clearing and stepped into a winter night warmed and unsettled by bonfires of burning trees—popping embers hissed and swarmed thick and threatening as yellow bees. Black smoke made invisible by the night invaded our throats, settled inside us like an unwelcome truth.

But that first summer here, migrant workers filled the air with mariachi: "Lo Dudo," "Soy Infeliz," "Un Amor Mas Puro"—music we only half-understood. We sat on the hill in the blue shadow of the white house and looked down on the red bandanas and brown backs below where the green trembled as callused hands reached in and stripped inferior fruit—diseased, wormed, or stunted—from every quivering limb.

We walked down into the trees and searched for something they might have missed. You found one peach—perfect, ripened early, its downy skin sloughing off as your thumb tested it and its honey seeped into your palm. We shared it and I took the nectar from your lips and chin and chest. And the sun set, sifting gold into the West.

But on the last night, firelight showed ragged rows of upturned soil where the declining trees had once grown, illuminated the thin fingers of feeder roots still reaching for their severed trunks. We had not touched each other for months. You coughed, leaned closer. I prayed that you would reach for me. But you pulled away, stared at the snowless, heat-cleared dirt, at the shattered burning trees, your eyes fixed on this wasting of life.

The Swan

For a month, on the way to work, I've passed
the pair of them—drifting side by side
on the black pond, never farther apart
than the breadth of a man's open arms.

Their beauty, now so often dismissed as trite,
is to my mind like the beauty of the rose—
its light witnessed so often, we no longer see it.
But this morning, there is one lone swan

chalked on the surface of the black water.
Should I be surprised? There is the proximity
of the pond to the heavily traveled road,
the stray dogs and silver foxes

in the surrounding pinewoods. Is it possible
that a white arrow of wings passed overhead,
just minutes before, calling out to the one
and not the other—a simple parting of ways?

There are so many possible explanations
for this separation. Why will none of them
console me?

Snow falls in Hartsville
For J.

1.

and to keep those considered to be children safe
at home, the high school shuts down. Now
the yellow buses won't slide into guard rails.
My girlfriend and I ride with my older sister
to the college where we promise to spend the day
in the library, learning things we could never learn
at home. She leaves us with the keys, goes on to class.
And we do learn—but not from books, not in the library,
but in the front seat of my sister's Dodge, idling,
as its white metal hood disappears in the torn paper
sky. My girl and I, just fifteen on turquoise
vinyl skin, heater blowing on the glass, our hands
inside each other's jeans, my skin inside hers,
windows milking white, snow becoming rain.

2.

Windows milking white, snow becoming rain,
warmer now inside her, and her hand sliding up
and down me, my fingers slipping into her,
melting. Both of us melting. Though I'm not sure
what to do with this mess on our hands—
I'm happier than I've ever been, coming
in her grip, in my jeans, because the only time
I'd come in someone's hand it was a strange
man's hand. I wanted so much to be
normal like my brother, like my father. Normal
like my girl. And there, protected from the snow,
sheltered by the Dodge, I found normal in my girl.
I didn't know then, that by the age of ten she could play,
by memory, "Dust in the Wind" on a Gibson guitar.

3.

She played "Dust in the Wind" on a Gibson guitar
her uncle had given her when she was younger
than ten—her uncle who'd been giving
her gifts since the day before she was born, and
molesting her since before she could talk.
This uncle with a thick beard and a thicker
gut called her *Short Stuff*, gave her
softball bats and gloves, taught her to be hard,
to fight like a man, to swing like a man, go down
on a man, take anything thrown her way, take him
every time. And she did follow through on every
curve he threw, knowing she would be struck out.
And even when she hit, the force of her own arm
twisted her into dirt. This was long before I loved her.

4.

Before I'd loved her long, dirt about her
family was all over town. Parents divorced,
smoking pot, letting their kids run wild
in a small country town where whole congregations
prayed on your sins, made sure you remained
the subject of shaming charity. I knew
her family wasn't any good, wasn't saved, and I,
the preacher's son, didn't care—I knew none of us
were saved the moment I sank to my knees
for the son of a farmer in the fields I played in
after school. I knew none of us were good
at being anything other than we are, no matter
how much we fight ourselves, each other, God—
we all end up on our knees in ways we never dreamed.

5.

We never dreamed we'd end up on our knees
together on her narrow bed when we were sixteen
and her parents were wherever her parents went
when they should have been beside her. And mine
were where I should have been—at home,
but I ran away to be with her, to prove
I was a man inside of her, my girl. And she was
so willing and soft, but it hurt her too much
in ways I wouldn't understand until
a year later, when I lay on my back
in my male lover's trailer in the longleaf pines
and took him inside me and remembered
how young I was when the farmer's son
had done to me what her uncle had done to her.

6.

But nothing done to me or done to her
made us what we truly are or even most of what
we were. I loved her because she was the first
man who loved me too. The first man, at least inside
her bones, who accepted the boy who couldn't be
a proper man, who couldn't be what he wanted
to be. And she played the Gibson guitar for me
and sang about what would eventually be
today—her short, strong fingers on the fret,
her soft breasts gone, removed by the hip
of the wood, music coming from two bellies
into mine. Only in some ways part of a gift
from the uncle who abused her. Where would we be
now if we'd confessed? But that was years ago.

7.

Twenty-five years ago, and counting still, she confessed
in a letter, not from my girl—but from the man
that she's become, the man she was always meant to be.
And it wasn't just the surgeries, it was years
of swinging hard and sometimes connecting
with the pitch—from *his* uncle, from *his* girlfriends,
and once or twice, from me. Now, I'd like to believe
I'm the man I was always meant to be—leaning in
to my lover, to my life, to the wonder
of having once been a man who loved a woman
who was almost the perfect man for me. But maybe
neither of us is done with becoming what we were
meant to be. No way to know. And still no way
to keep those considered to be children safe.

III.

I Have to Have You Like She Had to Have the Rain

With the purple juice of pokeweed
I paint the symbol of the twins
on my brow and walk into the fields.

Round and round I circle your memory,
your image—you naked and you free,
conjured in my head and heart. I sing

the song grandmother sang when
seedling corn was threatened by drought:

The clouds are sheep.
The winds are shepherds.
Shepherds, bring your sheep to me.

Round and round I circle you.
Louder and louder until the hum

of my lips trembles my cheeks and
all the while, I see the shorn, silver
hair of grandmother lifting in the wind

that brought the rain, the tassels of her shawl
quivering as shepherds undressed her,
the calico of her fallen apron darkening

as the flock descended, her naked feet
forging a circle of water around
the infant corn.

The Witch's Tree

Take my hand and we will go across
the black-water, roadside ditches wriggling
with the larvae of mosquitoes and the tadpoles

of toads. We will go over the rusted tracks
into the field of rain-soaked blackberries
and fragrant ferns. When we reach the witch's

tree our waists will be wet from walking with
the grasping gods of the afternoon. We will cast
off this world's weavings, crawl inside the oak,

curl our backs against her mossy walls, fasten
our mouths onto some verdant vine and suckle
side by side like twins sharing the womb.

Landscaper's Curse

We take a side street,
stroll left off Friendly Avenue
down blocks of well-kept bungalows—
first homes for couples better off
than us, painted in colors that intimate
quirky wines in wrought iron racks,
wardrobed TVs, loaves of rosemary bread
and cheeseboards on recycled countertops.
Coveting their lives, thinking
of our cave-like apartment
with its doll's oven you couldn't
roast a chicken in, I bitch about airs,
pretensions, unused herb gardens
just for show until we pass into the shadow
of a tree dressed for an evening party—
its every branch strung with seedpods
like tiny lanterns, pendulous hearts
of rice paper luminous as caressed skin. Its beauty
is damaging. I console myself by conjuring
an unflattering image of its owner—
a gaunt yuppie with no knowledge
of the tree's rarity, no awareness
of its magic, someone you couldn't love
the way you love me—
my landscaper's back broad and brown
from years of moving the earth. Someone
who couldn't share the drunken hours
after work, babbling plant lore,
piedmont clay still reddening his jeans,
until you've had enough
and pull him to bed. But tonight, before sleep,
I will curse the imagined
owner of that tree. I will whisper
Koelreuteria bipinnata.
Even the name is a spell
on the tongue of those
who know how to say it.

A Rumor of Fire

Ragged August—a wounded month
slinks under the house, panting in the crawlspace.

Dogwoods burn red two months early.
Birds roost in midday, feverish and thin

as thorns. Lawns singe to thatch brittle
as old doll hair—a rumor of fire

could reduce the neighborhood to ash. I draw the blinds
against the struggle. The air conditioner labors

in darkness. The house is small—
two bedrooms, one bath, a narrow living

room—all we could afford. Six years ago we signed off
in the cool of spring—the front yard masted

with pines, billowed by one live oak,
foam white camellias cresting the blue door. The walls

seemed conceptual, as if longing could sail
us beyond them into the garden. Now I lie

on the sofa, the low ceiling trapping my breath
like a mask, and realize I have never lived

in a house I have loved. I want to wake up
in a soft bed, in a room so vast the walls are imagined,

windows flung wide as the horizon, rain falling
in the green world. And you, my love,

I want you to emerge like a seedling
from the furrowed sheets, dazzled and new,

watching for the rising storm within me.

In the Tattoo Parlor

Hide it on your shoulder, baby, just beneath your sleeve,
she says. *You won't be young forever and there's nothing attractive*
about ink fading on old skin—

as if decades from now, she would treasure the natural grace
of his unmarked skin or look lovingly
on his inkless age-deflated arm surrendering the past

of muscles flooded with blood, the wanton nights
of moonlight across the hard curve of his shoulder.

She leans into his body as they flip through books
of black symbols.

When her hand reaches up and straightens the back
of his striped t-shirt, I want to think her prejudice
is one of perfect pattern and line:

that she prefers her linens un-rumpled, her photos scrap-booked
and creaseless, her garden in rows—but the halter she wears
of accordioned flowers that her breasts don't stretch smooth

tells me it's not the thought of a wrinkled tattoo on her lover's skin
that grieves her.

And I know someday, sooner than she suspects, her own skin shirred
like the curtains of a hearse, she'll look into the mirror, unable to recall
the girl that shopped tattoos with her man one August night.

For all of its windows

the cardiologist's waiting room is dark—
the smoked glass won't allow
the outside in. The other patients
hunch in their chairs like caged doves.

When I was a child,
my father made paper airplanes for me
when it was too cold to play outside.
The rooms filled with his paper birds,
and the ceiling of our small, rented house
opened like the sky.

After the Storm

Graveyard flowers litter Shipyard Boulevard—petals of plastic and silk, stems of stiff wire. As we pass over the wind's wreckage, you stare through the passenger window and say, *Sad. I wonder who picks them all up?* I would answer the obvious—inmates on work detail, a road crew, the caretakers—but you're not asking about jobs and duties. I know you; you're wondering who these men are inside, whether it grieves them to gather these tattered bits of color into black bags and toss them away as if they hadn't been picked by fingers opened by loss. As if they weren't mementos of what finally—when the last loved-one visits and we are never tended to again—becomes of us all. For you, I want to be the man who knows which garish bouquet goes where, who brakes in the middle of the street, door flung wide, stops traffic, then peels each false leaf from the asphalt, gathers them all until the last fake flower is whole again and tucked respectfully back into the smooth green blanket so carefully drawn over the dead. Or better yet: for you, I want to be the kind of man who sees this sad morning as the evidence of a blossoming, or the fallen confetti of a parade—as if the dead woke during the storm, threw back the covers, and danced in flowers and thunder until the sun came up.

Lost

Dredged awake in darkness
by the foghorn of a slow barge
on the Cape Fear and the whistle-yawn
of the dog at my feet—
and I remember my lover fell asleep
on the couch again
last night and did not come
to bed. Nothing to do
with fighting, no anger,
just a decade or so since first love,
and now too much work,
and the fact that I've begun to snore
like an old man. Sunrise will be
a long time coming and there is no need
to look past the open window—
the air is thick and damp
inside the bedroom—there will be nothing
to see beyond the reach
of the streetlamp's yellow beard. *Listen
instead, lost boy, to find your way
into this morning.* Listen
to the groan of steel on the river—
almost too much weight,
almost blind, but calling out
to someone who worries and watches,
who listens because
he's paid to. Listen
and hear the stretching jaw
as the whine rises in your mind,
a guiding pillar of cloud
that leads you deep inside
the black throat. And know
these are only two of the sounds
of sleeplessness and of waking.
Somewhere, someone you love
is turning in the darkness,

in the fog. Somewhere, someone
softly breathing turns his face
into the pillow, slips back into sleep
and forgets you.

Nature Sounds
For Ben

It seemed a godsend—an alarm clock programmed with nature sounds. Something to drown out my snoring and quiet your work stress now that the oscillating fan I'd had since we met (the one that once cooled the sweat of our bodies after lovemaking) had just died. We tried them all—*Birds of the Forest* (too raucous for sleep, and you've been afraid of birds since paleontologists called them flying dinosaurs), *Lapping Waves* (too repetitious, like the ocean snoring), *Mountain Waterfall* (too urgent a lullaby, too demanding a mother). We chose *Gentle Shower.* There'd been no rain in months and even its recorded whisper was better than the long silence of drought. But sometimes I hear a pattern—every few seconds it loops back and I know whoever digitalized the rain only spared a moment of their workday to capture it. Still, most nights it seems real enough and masks the sounds of our growing older. And who can fault a clock that lulls you to sleep with a gentle shower, keeps the time, wakes you faithfully at 5 am for work, for having a memory too small to recall an entire night of rain?

When you touch me

you lay hands
on the bones of lovers
I lost years ago.
You conjure
desires not entirely
my own.

When you stroke
my thigh, your hand
is guided by the hands
of these others—
a Ouija scrawling

the answer to the question
that still roams
the dark husk
of our house: *love you?*
yes,

we love you.

Lost Boy

Sometimes sex is like grasping the velvet trunks of sumac, hearing the crunch of that year's weeds, that fall's skeletons beneath my tender knees, and it returns me to thirteen. Slender ribs of childhood protruding from the memory-mulch of maple twigs, cicada skins, pine-straw puncturing like needles reminding me of the morning the stranger took what I didn't give.

Sometimes these bones of youth run me through when you do, and I shudder in the sheets—somehow still a wounded thing, clawing remembered roots of sumac trees, reaching for a safe and quiet place— urged on by the boy I was forced to shed. And yet

there is so much in what you're doing now I *do* need—something even back then, when he first tore down my pants and I scratched and clawed into the mix of earth and leaves and badger tracks. So much now in the way you hold my hips—I believe I asked for then, or why would I have followed him into the thicket?

If I could, half of me would go back to the woods, and the man I am now would kill the stranger where he stands—his cock still hard as he nervously wipes the boy's blood from his hands onto his red t-shirt before fastening his pants without a word for the boy in the leaves who wants to die.

And yet, that half of me remains here, with you, my love, almost happy to leave the boy where he still lies, and almost grateful for the ecstasy of what you're doing.

Red Horse

Most nights, the boy grooms the red horse.
Most days the boy re-bags the trash
in the cinderblock pit by the road.

Both have to be done so he doesn't complain,
though the horse is a only dream, and the pit is his
town's way of dealing with trash.

His true nature is beautiful—a long-necked statue
precariously left on the picnic table. One night
while strapping the mane of the red horse,

the boy sees the statue tip and fall from the table.
There is a hairline crack from chin to sternum.
He uprights it again, more carefully, but still

he is broken. The red horse will never forgive him.
Weeks pass before the town sends its trucks
to the country. In that time the rain

and sun melt the black plastic and the trash
festers, is riddled with maggots. The boy
takes up his shovel and five new bags,

prays he will unearth the broken statue
in the pit. There is a neighbor boy who is older—he waits
on the back porch swing, his cock is always hard.

Some nights, some days, the boys groom each other
when the red horse won't come or when the crop duster
does and the fields by the road are unsafe. Sometimes

the crop duster half-moons over the porch, nearly stalls,
engine like a chainsaw as it turns back to the melon fields.
Another pass. The stench is all over them

now. The red horse can't always be returned to.
The broken statue never returns. The boy
with the shovel no longer digs for it.

Answering emails at 5 am

and my dogs, blood dreaming in their hearts,
padding across a cold barren in Mongolia,
bounding into the half-frozen sea off Labrador,

are in reality sprawled across my legs, giving
and getting only what they must, doing
what I should be doing by doing so

very little. The sun will rise before 7—a salmon
flash beyond the black river of the tree line
with its ice-trapped banks of blacker leaves. By then

I will be writing this poem, another attempt
to make sense of why I am never doing
what I should when I should—which is to say

while I can. Last evening, driving home,
I saw the shadows of two strangers
walking through the scrubby field I pass

twice daily. I know this scrap of land
only at a distance and from traveling past
it at 50 miles an hour, but even passing

I know it as a refuge for goslings of soft broom
sedge and their parents, necks like handless black
walking sticks. And I know it to be a haven

in summer for the wild blue salvia that hazes the ground
like a low noon sky until the twilight morning
glories overcome it and bind it below their undulating

beauty. Someday, some night, I'll get it right and stop
in the middle of the street, get out and become
a black shadow that is also a black river that knows

what it knows and asks nothing else, as it treads on
sky until night turns cold—and it heads home on foot
and lies down like the full moon just before dawn, contented,

across its master's thighs.

Late Morning in Oakdale Cemetery

Finally the oldest and weakest coffin
collapses with a subterranean sigh

as a rectangular cave-in of moist earth
completes a burial long overdue.

Now the browning flower can fall
from the bough of the japonica

into the open hand of the stone
angel that still prays.

And the moment after the caretaker
mows the graveyard lawn,

even the grass can lick its wounds
and get on with the business of life.

Everything is possible

here, in this room of open windows
and metal screens that sieve the morning light
and birdsong, where there exists another window
across your knees
            that is also a screen of light
upon which you can type and still hear the words
of the girl who sings from Yorkshire *and we'll all go*
together, to pull wild mountain thyme, all around
the blooming heather.
          And through the screen of metal
just above the sofa, behind your back, threads the song
of a mockingbird just feet away, who has no song
of his own, but makes a life of conjuring voices
he's heard—some of them just this day, some of them recalled
and resurrected from when he was young
and seasons and miles away.

Everything is possible
in this world of open screens that contain and emit the light
of the Yorkshire girl who sings in a fading house of brick and clay
so many miles away, this house which is also a recording
studio where her younger brother,
                shoulders silk-screened
with angel's wings, mixes this moment of her voice,
with the recent past of a guitar, that rests now, so silent,
in its black case. Everything is possible
            in this world
where lives are recorded in the moment—gunfire
and ambulances, students and teachers running
on the palm-sized screen of a shaking cell
phone, a child smiling up at her mother through
an ever-changing picture in its gilded frame
that becomes a sun rising
          over a house never to be returned to.

Still,
    in this world of open screens, nearly everything
can be remembered, because there is also a benevolent librarian,
made of light, who files away the seconds, the minutes, the hours,
even the years now stacked behind you like shelves
in the darkening rooms of your past.
                        Though some memories,
you know, are lost, misfiled, because as devoted to your history
as this librarian is, she, like you, is sometimes distracted
by music and by luminous updates from the future.
Or by posts from friends so many miles away, like this one
that came today from Argentina
                    it is warm & brilliantly clear,
winds from the northeast in the afternoon. off to ride horses
in the sand.

About the Author

Daniel Nathan Terry, a former landscaper and horticulturist, is the author of *Capturing the Dead* (NFSPS 2008), which won The Stevens Prize, and a chapbook, *Days of Dark Miracles* (Seven Kitchens Press 2011). His poetry has appeared, or is forthcoming, in many journals and anthologies, including *New South, Poet Lore, Assaracus, Chautauqua,* and *Collective Brightness.* He teaches English at the University of North Carolina Wilmington and serves on the advisory board of One Pause Poetry.

About the cover artist

Benjamin Billingsley is a painter and printmaker living in Wilmington, North Carolina, with his husband, poet Daniel Nathan Terry. He holds an MFA from UNC Greensboro, and has exhibited work in the Southeastern United States as well as in Estonia, Russia and Japan. Ben is the third generation artist and art instructor in his family. In 2006 Benjamin Billingsley received the Marilyn Goodman Anderson Endowed Award for Excellence in Teaching. His artwork has appeared in several publications, including full-length book *...hide behind me...*(Main Street Rag 2011) from poet and novelist, Jason Mott.

More of his work can be viewed at www.benjaminbillingsley.com .

CPSIA information can be obtained at www.ICGtesting.com
Printed in the USA
LVOW061446070712

289151LV00004B/16/P